# Astro Academy

'Astro Academy'
An original concept by Cath Jones
© Cath Jones

Illustrated by Max Rambaldi

**Published by MAVERICK ARTS PUBLISHING LTD**
Studio 11, City Business Centre, 6 Brighton Road,
Horsham, West Sussex, RH13 5BB
© Maverick Arts Publishing Limited November 2020
+44 (0)1403 256941

A CIP catalogue record for this book is available at the British Library.

**ISBN 978-1-84886-723-9**

www.maverickbooks.co.uk

This book is rated as: White Band (Guided Reading)

# Astro Academy

By Cath Jones

Illustrated by Max Rambaldi

# Chapter 1

It was Abdi's first day at his new school, Abbey Academy. He ran down the road towards the school bus stop. Suddenly, he spotted a minibus.

"Wait for me!" he yelled.

He hurled himself at the open doors, tripped on the step and fell into the bus. **WHOOSH!**

The doors closed behind him. Abdi collapsed panting into an empty seat.

"Hi," said a voice. "I'm Sash. I've not seen you before."

Abdi jerked round in surprise and stared at the girl. "Hi," he said. "I'm Abdi."

"First day at the Academy?" she asked. Abdi nodded. "You only just caught the bus!"

The driver interrupted with a loud shout, "Seatbelts please. Launching in 5 seconds…"

Abdi clicked his seatbelt in. "What does he mean 'launching'?" he asked.

But before Sash could reply, there was a tremendous roaring sound. Then the minibus tilted back! Abdi yelped in alarm and hung onto his seat. The roaring grew louder and louder. The minibus began to shake.

"Blast off!" the other pupils whooped excitedly. Abdi closed his eyes as the minibus launched forwards. He concentrated on not being sick. This was worse than a fairground ride!

Suddenly, it went calm.

"We have left Earth's atmosphere!" yelled the driver.

"Left Earth?!" Abdi repeated in alarm.

"Docking in 3-2-1," continued the driver. There was a thud and the minibus jerked forward. Then everything was still.

"What's going on?" asked Abdi.

A door slid open and a tall woman in a smart uniform strode onto the bus.

"Welcome back to Astro Academy," she said.

"*Astro* Academy," Abdi murmured in disbelief. "I'm supposed to be going to *Abbey* Academy! I must have caught the wrong minibus!"
Sash stared at Abdi with a worried expression.
"What's Astro Academy?" Abdi asked.

"Astro Academy is space school," Sash said.

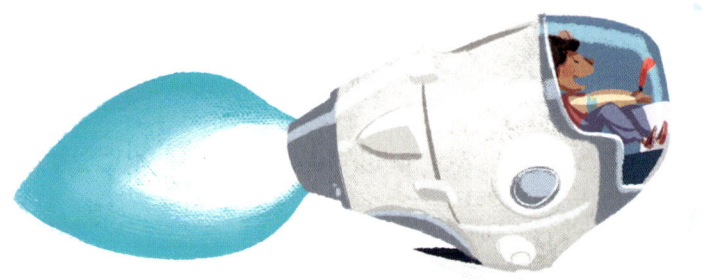

# Chapter 2

Abdi gazed round the classroom. His head was spinning with questions.

"Am I really in space?" he asked in a shaky voice. "And are you all *aliens?*"

The pupils nodded.

"But you don't look any different to humans," he whispered.

Sash smiled. "Our parents are stationed on Earth. We need to blend in."

One of the pupils stepped forward and frowned at Abdi. "You'll be in big trouble if Captain Mills works out you're a human!"

"Kresh!" said Sash. "Don't frighten Abdi."

"Well, Captain Mills doesn't like mistakes. Astro Academy is meant to be top secret!" Kresh said.

Sash smiled reassuringly at Abdi. "We'll hide you until home time. Just stay close and copy everything we do. You're in luck! Frank didn't catch the bus this morning, and you look a bit like him. So today *you* can be Frank."

Suddenly, Kresh whispered, "Captain Mills is coming!"

Abdi leapt up and hid behind Sash. He peered out nervously at the woman he'd seen on the bus.

"Hello students," she said. "Welcome back to your second year at Astro Academy. Today will be your first day of *Space Pod Training*." She held out a tray with lots of wristbands. "Students will be required to wear a locator at all times. This is to make sure we don't lose you in space. Unauthorised removal will result in a trip to my office and a letter to your parents."

Abdi copied everyone else and clipped a band onto his left wrist. It felt slightly warm.

"Follow me!" ordered Captain Mills.

# Chapter 3

Captain Mills took the register in the space pod bay.

"Frank Drake?" she called. There was a pause.

"That's you," Sash whispered.

"Present!" Abdi yelped.

The captain gave Abdi a hard stare. "Did you get a haircut, Frank?"

"Um, yes Captain!" Abdi panicked. The captain raised her eyebrows and went back to the register. Abdi let out a sigh of relief.

Ten minutes later, Abdi was sitting alone in the pilot seat of a space pod. 'I can't fly a spaceship!' he thought. The explanation Captain Mills had given was all nonsense to him.

Sash was sitting in a space pod next to him. She was trying to tell him to fake a stomach ache and get out, but she stopped suddenly. Captain Mills knocked on the top of Abdi's pod.

"Frank, why haven't you taken off yet?" she demanded.

Abdi swung round in panic and caught his elbow on a red button. There was a swooshing sound as the doors locked. Above him, the captain was waving her hands and mouthing something, but Abdi couldn't hear anything she was saying.

Without warning, a row of lights flashed on the control panel and the engine began to roar.

Abdi leant forward to press the button again, hoping to stop the space pod. But he caught his sleeve on the control stick. The space pod shot forward!

"Oh no!" Abdi grabbed the control stick and soon discovered that it was just like playing on his computer at home. Flying a space pod was amazing!

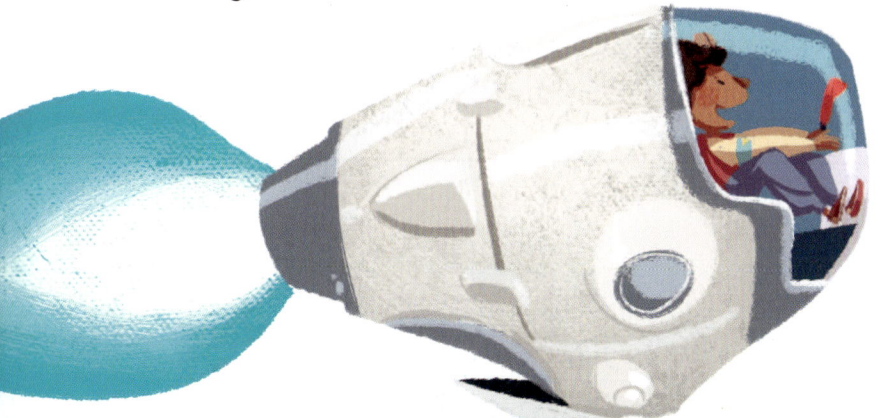

Half an hour later, Abdi landed and emerged from the space pod. Captain Mills strode up to him. Abdi closed his eyes. This was it: the moment of discovery.

"Congratulations," the captain said. Abdi looked up in surprise. "That was a sensational first flight. You flew for 30 minutes and successfully docked with the mother ship. You're a natural!"

"Uh, thank you," said Abdi.

At that moment, the end of lesson bell sounded.

"Good work, Frank!" Sash said with a big wink.

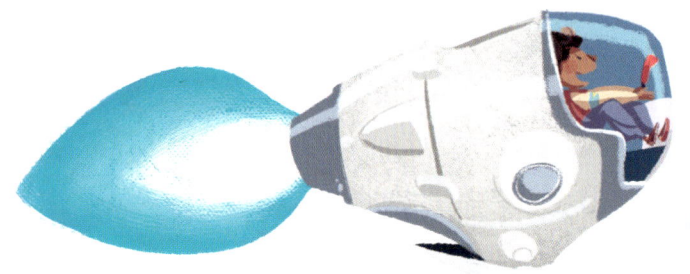

# Chapter 4

Abdi peered at Sash's timetable. "What's next?" he asked.

"The Zero Gravity Zone!" Sash grinned.

It didn't take long for everyone to change into padded suits. Abdi snickered. They all looked as if they had been pumped up by a bicycle pump! The room hummed with excited whispers as the captain clapped her hands for quiet.

"In a moment, you will enter the Space Tank." She gestured towards a large, glass-sided room. "As you know, it's a Zero Gravity Zone. Unlike the rest of the ship, gravity technology does not operate in there. You will be split into teams to play a game. The first team to get the ball into the net wins."

Sash and Abdi were both in Red Team. Abdi stood back as everyone dived through the entrance door. They cheered and giggled as they started floating.

Abdi tingled with excitement. But as soon as he entered, he tripped! He waved his arms like a crazy windmill, trying to remain upright, but it was no good. He somersaulted across the tank! Within seconds, he was floating next to Sash.

The tank filled with laughter as everyone tried to reach the ball. But it was almost impossible not to float past it.

Abdi flapped his arms, kicked his legs and wobbled his bottom. This sent him floating sideways! Suddenly, the ball bounced into his stomach which sent him bumping into Sash. They hooted with laughter as they spun straight into the net!

"Red team win!" shouted Captain Mills. "Well done, Frank."

# Chapter 5

Finally, it was home time. The students removed their locators and put them back on the tray. Abdi had had such a fantastic day. He felt a bit glum about the thought of starting at Abbey Academy.

"Time to catch the minibus!" Sash said. "You're almost home, Abdi."

"Oh yeah... Better make sure I catch the right one this time!"

As they boarded to go home, Sash laughed. "I don't think we did a very good job of keeping you hidden!"

Abdi grinned. It was true. He had caused quite a commotion!

"Buckle up and prepare for launch!" the driver announced.

"I wish I could come back here," Abdi admitted. "Astro Academy is amazing."

Sash gave Abdi a hug. "I'm sorry Abdi. We'll miss you."

The engines roared and Abdi felt the floor

vibrate gently beneath his feet.

"5-4-3-2..." chanted the pupils.

Suddenly the engines fell silent.

"Open the doors!" shouted a loud voice. Abdi's heart raced in alarm as the captain walked in. "You forgot something, *Abdi*," she said. She knew his name! Abdi swallowed nervously. "Here," she said and handed Abdi his Abbey Academy backpack, with his name on the label.

"Oops," said Abdi. He expected to get told off, but the captain just smiled.

"Have a good trip home," she said.

★★★

The next morning, Abdi arrived at the bus stop nice and early. When the minibus pulled up, he read the destination out loud twice, just to be sure. "Abbey Academy, Abbey Academy."

He sighed and stepped onto the minibus.

He was going to miss Sash and the other students, and the cool lessons.

Suddenly, the minibus erupted with the sound of shouting and whooping. "Surprise!"

Abdi was shocked to see Sash and the whole Astro Academy class!

"Sash!" Abdi gasped in delight. "What are you doing here?"

Before Sash could reply, Captain Mills stepped forward. Abdi gulped nervously.

"Abdi, I am pleased to tell you that Astro Academy would like to offer you a scholarship. We want you to be an official student at our school."

Abdi could hardly believe his ears. It was a dream come true! He shook Captain Mills's hand.

"I would be honoured!" he beamed.

## The End

# Book Bands for Guided Reading

The Institute of Education book banding system is a scale of colours that reflects the various levels of reading difficulty. The bands are assigned by taking into account the content, the language style, the layout and phonics. Word, phrase and sentence level work is also taken into consideration.

Maverick Early Readers are a bright, attractive range of books covering the pink to white bands. All of these books have been book banded for guided reading to the industry standard and edited by a leading educational consultant.

To view the whole Maverick Readers scheme, visit our website at
www.maverickearlyreaders.com

Or scan the QR code above to view our scheme instantly!